Easy Peasy Lemon Squeezy

Recipes by
Jo Seagar

Cartoons by
John Stringer

RANDOM HOUSE
NEW ZEALAND

DEDICATED TO ALL **PARENTS & GRANDPARENTS**
SEEKING WAYS TO MAKE COOKING
FUN, SIMPLE & EASY FOR CHILDREN

AND ALSO TO KATE & GUY,
THE WORLD'S BEST BOWL AND SPOON LICKERS,
AND ASH, JAMES & ALEX,
WHO ENDURED DAD'S APRICOT AND SPINACH
AMORPHOUS BLOB FROM OUTER SPACE

Hi, I'm Jo, keepin' an eye on Gordon, Hot Dog and especially Rooky to make sure everything is cookin'. I'm the oil that holds this kitchen gang together.
Gordon Bleu (Blaagh) bringing you whizzo treats and advice from the finest cookery school in the world. OK, so I like wearing a hat that looks like a cauliflower - s'better than cauliflower ears! - what could be wurst?
'Hot Dog!' Being a sausage dog from a long line of dachshunds - that can trace a lineage back to the Great Banger, a German Shepherd (pie) - I gotta sniff around and make sure this lot make a dog's breakfast of everything. Cheerio!
Yo Dudes! Rooky Cook, I jez ollie right into the kitchen with Jo 'n' Gordon to learn whatever I can about food and cookin'. (A) cos I like food (what ado...adoeshent adoleeshment..."teenager" doesn't?) and (B) cos being a slick cook seems to impress girls majorly.

Introduction for the owner of this book

I love cooking. It's what I do for my job and for my hobby.

The reason I am so passionate about cooking is that it is simple and achievable. It really isn't very hard to learn to cook and once you understand the special words associated with it (baking, grilling, etc) and have mastered the basic techniques then the rest is easy. I was never very good at maths at school but with cooking I found I could easily follow a recipe and I loved making something – especially something to eat!

We have included some important stuff at the front of the book. While cooking is fun, the kitchen can be hazardous. That's why we've written the safety bits and pieces – read through the rules before you get into the fun part – the cooking. If you have any problems, ask an adult to help.

Also at the back are a glossary and an index. Like most businesses or hobbies, cooking has developed a special set of words and the glossary sets out some of these words that are used in our recipes and explains what they mean. This is just a starter list but should be sufficient at this stage. Use the index to find a particular recipe.

Let us know at www.ezpzcook.com what you think of the book, what your favourite recipes are and send us other recipes that you like making and you think could do with the John Stringer cartoon treatment. Happy cooking and enjoy your wonderful results.

Jo Seagar

Introduction for adults

John and I have produced the 'EZPZ Cook' cartoons because we both have a passion for cooking and we both have kids in the 'tweenie' stage – not teenagers yet but they're too big to be little kids. They love to cook and help in the kitchen – chopping vegetables, stirring saucepans and spooning out muffins don't even rate as chores to them. We need to encourage this useful activity and they are desperate to learn – and of course eat the results.

Cooking together is great family time. The recipes we've got in *Easy Peasy Lemon Squeezy*, this first collection of the 'EZPZ Cook' cartoon strips, are all really easy to make. Your kids will be successful with these recipes – that has to be good for their confidence and self esteem. They also get something to eat at the end of it!

While the kids ought to be able to make all these things on their own, remember the kitchen can be hazardous for children. We've put in some information about safety in the kitchen. We've tried to word this in a positive way, not a list of DON'TS – if this is going to be fun, then the whole experience needs to be fun, even understanding the rules.

Which brings you to the hardest part . . . keeping your cool when it comes to tidying up. Neither John nor I like this part either, but then we both have wonderful spouses so we can get out of it. What's a little mess after all!

Have a great time with this, we're looking forward to hearing your reaction and ideas at www.ezpzcook.com.

Jo Seagar

Safety in the kitchen

Cooking is great fun but it includes lots of heat and the use of sharp knives and appliances. Below are some basic rules for you to follow to help make sure your cooking is safe as well as fun.

General

1. Always ask an adult's permission before cooking.
2. Before starting the recipe, read it through and make sure you have all the ingredients and the equipment you will need.
3. Wear an apron to keep your clothes clean.
4. Wash your hands. You're going to put this food into your mouth so you don't want dirt in it.
5. Keep long hair tied back and roll up your sleeves.
6. Make sure the stovetop is clear of tea towels and mitts and cookbooks.
7. Being tidy and neat can prevent accidents – wash dirty tools as you finish with them and wipe up spills immediately to prevent skids.

Ovens & stovetops

These guys are serious pieces of equipment.

1. If the racks in the oven need height adjusting, do this before you turn the oven on.
2. When opening the oven door, stand back so that the hot steam can escape before you try to remove anything. If you wear glasses, be careful as your glasses may fog up.
3. Always use oven mitts when taking things out of the oven. Make sure they are dry – if you use anything damp, the heat will go straight through and burn your hand. (The heat from the tray will boil the water in the damp cloth, just like water in an electric kettle).
4. Keep pot handles pointing to the side so that no-one can knock them and tip the contents over themselves or you.
5. Make sure pot handles are not over another element or burner as the handle will heat up and give you a bad burn when you try to pick it up.
6. Turn the element or burner off before removing a pot or pan from the stovetop.
7. Ask an adult to drain foods cooked in lots of water, such as pasta. Pans full of water are heavy and wobble a lot. If not done right the water and the steam could burn you.
8. Remember to turn everything off when you are finished.

Electrical appliances

1. Never use wet hands to switch on or to plug in anything electrical. Check that the machine is switched off before you turn on the power at the wall.
2. Turn off the mixer or processor before reaching into the mixing bowl. Never reach into the bowl with your hands or try to scrape the sides of the bowl with a spatula while the mixer is still running.
3. Turn off the electric beater and be sure it is unplugged before you put the beaters in or take them out.
4. Turn off the blender before removing the lid. Blenders with the lid off act like geysers! Never put your hands into a blender or try to scrape the sides with a spatula while the blender is still running.

Knives and other sharp tools

1. Don't hold things and cut them – put them down on a chopping board. If you're cutting something that is round, like an onion, cut it in half first and then put it on the chopping board flat-side down.
2. Hold the knife firmly and handle it with care – don't fool around with knives.
3. Always cut with the blade pointing away from you.
4. Wash knives and sharp tools individually. If you put them in a sink full of soapy water, you or someone else could reach in and grab a blade or sharp edge by mistake.

Microwaves

1. Be careful not to burn yourself. Even though microwaves go right through containers without heating them, the hot food inside can make the container hot.
2. Microwaved food keeps cooking after you take it out of the oven. Let it cool for a few minutes before eating.

Measuring

Rooky Cook and Gordon Bleu want to make cooking easy peasy! They have tried to make sure that measurements are in cups or teaspoons or tablespoons.

Cups  Officially a cup is 250 ml. For cooking, plastic measuring cups are great. The main thing is to use the same sort of cup – switching to Granny's good tea cups is not a good idea.

TSP/tsp Teaspoon. Again, use the same type of teaspoon for all measures in the same recipe and you should be fine.

TBSP/tbsp Tablespoon. These are cooking or serving spoons and are bigger then the spoons you eat your dessert with.

Generally spoons and cups should be levelled off or at least not heaped up as high as they can be. We're not particularly strict about scientifically accurate measurements, especially when adding goodies like chocolate chips!

Easy Peasy Lemon Squeezy

Green
GHERKiN
DiP
INGREDIENTS
• 250 gm sour cream
• 3 tbsp pickle or gherkin relish
• 2 tbsp chopped parsley

YO, ROOKY COOK! WOULD YOU MIX THESE INGREDIENTS INTO A BOWL? (IT'S 'EZPZ LEMON SQUEEZY')
SURE, GORDON BLEU.. WE COULD SERVE THE DIP WITH RAW VEGES, CHIPS or CRACKER BISQUITS.
'HOT DOG!' WHY NOT SERVE AS A SAND-WICH FILLING, SPREAD ON TOAST or PIKELETS?

Useful Tip

Read a recipe all the way through to check you have everything you need – utensils and ingredients – before you begin.

"QUICKLY ADD RARE ART-ICHOKE INNERS FROM THE NIGERIAN HINTERLAND TO PREVENT THE PIE EXPLODING."
RUMBLE

PEANUT-BUTTER COOKIES
INGREDIENTS
2 CRUNCHY PEANUT-BUTTER
2 SUGAR
2 EGGS

ROOKY COOK, MIX THE INGREDIENTS UNTIL WELL COMBINED.
Roger, Gordon Bleu.

DROP SPOONFULS ON TO A GREASED OR BAKING PAPER-LINED TRAY
I like to flatten them with a fork.

BAKE AT 170 C (FAN-BAKE) FOR 10 MIN.
COOL ON A WIRE RACK.
MUMPH
CRUNCH

Useful Tip

Test if biscuits are done and cook them a little longer if necessary.

Easy Peasy Lemon Squeezy

LEMONADE SCONES
INGREDIENTS
• 4 SELF-RAISING FLOUR
• 300 ML CREAM (1 carton or small bottle)
• 1 CAN LEMONADE SPRITE or 7-UP
• 1/2 TSP SALT

MIX ALL INGREDIENTS IN A BOWL TO A SMOOTH DOUGH.

TIP OUT ON TO A WELL-FLOURED BENCH. CUT INTO SQUARES.

BAKE AT 220 C (FAN-BAKE) FOR 15-20 MIN. UNTIL GOLDEN. CHECK THEY ARE COOKED THRU.
COOL ON A RACK. SERVE WARM WITH JAM & WHIPPED CREAM.

Useful Tip

Dip the knife in flour before you cut scones to prevent it sticking to the mixture.

BACON &
POTATO
SERVES 4
FRITTATA
• 4 RASHES of RINDLESS BACON (chopped into small pieces)
• 3 MEDIUM POTATOES (scrubbed & cut into small 1 cm cubes)
• 3 TBSP CHOPPED PARSLEY
• 2 GRATED CHEESE
• 4 EGGS (beaten together)

FRY BACON IN A LITTLE OIL UNTIL CRISP.
STIR-FRY POTATO CUBES UNTIL SOFT (about 5 min)

STIR-IN PARSLEY, GRATED CHEESE & BEATEN EGGS. SEASON WITH SALT & PEPPER.

TURN DOWN HEAT & COOK 4 MIN. UNTIL BOTTOM IS CRISP & THE CENTRE IS SETTING.
TOP SHOULD BE WET & UNCOOKED.

PLACE PAN UNDER GRILL TO BROWN FOR 3-4 MIN.
Hot Dog!
CUT INTO WEDGES, SERVE IMMEDIATELY.

Useful Tip

Always keep eggs in the fridge. They will last longer and keep much fresher.

RARK!

JURASSIC SOUP ANYONE?

CHEESEY
FIELD MUSH-
ROOMS
YOU'RE NOT FROM CHESHIRE ARE YOU?
4 LARGE FLAT FIELD MUSHROOMS
1/2 GRATED CHEESE
APPROX. 4 TBSP CREAM CHEESE
2 TBSP CHIVES or SPRING ONIONS (Chopped)
1-2 CLOVES GARLIC (1/2 tsp crushed)
SERVES 4
REMOVE MUSHROOM STALKS & CHOP FINELY. MIX CHOPPED STALKS, CHEESE, CREAM CHEESE, CHIVES & GARLIC ALL TOGETHER. DIVIDE EVENLY BETWEEN 4 MUSHROOMS.
CHOP

PLACE UNDER A HOT ~~GORILLA~~ GRILLER & COOK APPROX. 12-15 MIN. UNTIL GOLDEN & CRISPY.
OOOK OOK OOOK
NEVER MONKEY WITH THE STOVE.
THEY CAN BE HEATED IN A MICROWAVE 2-3 MIN. ON HIGH (MUSHROOMS NOT GORILLAS).

Useful Tip

Microwaved food keeps cooking after you take it out of the oven. Let it cool for a few minutes before eating.

UNBELIEVABLE HAM + CHEESE PIE
60GM BUTTER (softened)
1 CHOPPED HAM
(or cooked sausage)
1 TBSP PARSLEY
1 GRATED CHEESE
1/2 FLOUR
SALT & PEP.
5 EGGS
1 CHOPPED ONION
"unbelievable" because it's so easy to make & cooks like a self-crusting quiche. No need to fiddle with a pastry layer first.
PUT FLOUR, EGGS & BUTTER IN A FOOD PROCESSOR or LARGE BOWL. PROCESS TO COMBINE.
RARGG!
CLIK

POUR EGG MIXTURE INTO A WELL-GREASED OR OIL-SPRAYED PIE PLATE.
TOP WITH HAM, ONION, SALT & PEPPER TO TASTE.
SPRINKLE WITH CHEESE.
BAKE AT 180 C 35-40 MIN. OR UNTIL MIXTURE IS SET & TOP IS GOLDEN BROWN. SPRINKLE WITH PARSLEY.
Serves 4
5-00

Useful Tip

If you're cutting something that is round, such as an onion, cut it in half first and then put it on the chopping board flat-side down.

MAKE 40
SIMPLE CHEESE STRAWS
•2 SHEETS THAWED PRE-ROLLED FROZEN PUFF/ FLAKY PASTRY
•GARLIC SALT
•1 GRATED TASTY CHEESE (Tip: keep a bag in the freezer. It never goes mouldy & can be used frozen).
PREHEAT OVEN TO 200 C. CUT PASTRY INTO STRIPS APPROX. 1 CM WIDE X 10 CM LONG.
Hot Dog! They look like French Fries!

PLACE ON A WELL-GREASED BAKING TRAY.
GARLIC
Place straws close together, but not quite touching.

Before baking, sprinkle with grated cheese & dust with garlic salt.
Bake for 8-10 min. until puffed-up, golden & crispy looking.

COOL ON A WIRE RACK & STORE IN AN AIRTIGHT CONTAINER. THEY ARE NICEST WARM (reheat in a low oven to warm & crisp up).
6-00

Useful Tip

Keep your rolling pin in the freezer till you need it, then flour won't stick to it.

FRENCH TOAST
INGREDIENTS
•2 EGGS
•1/2 MILK
•6 SLICES FRENCH (or toast-sliced) BREAD
•1/2 TSP CINNAMON
SERVES 6

BEAT EGGS, MILK & CINNAMON IN A BOWL.
Hot Dog!
DIP BREAD IN EGG MIXTURE.

Heat a non-stick frypan.
SPRAY GENEROUSLY WITH OIL OR MELT A LITTLE BUTTER IN THE PAN.
FRY BREAD SLICES (don't have pan too hot).

WHEN GOLDEN, TURN THEM OVER. Yum!
EAT WITH A SQUIRT OF MAPLE OR GOLDEN SYRUP & FRESH FRUIT.
12·00

Useful Tip

When measuring out golden syrup or treacle, run the spoon under hot water first – it warms the liquid and makes it easier to run off.

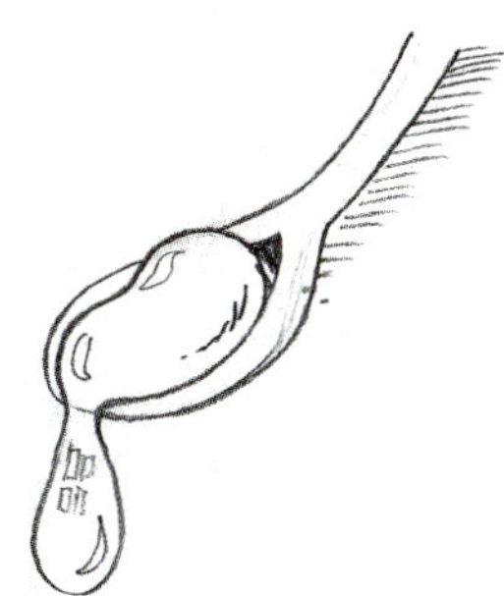

Easy Peasy Lemon Squeezy

EZPZ MACARONI CHEEZEY
1 ONION (CHOPPED FINELY)
1 CUP GRATED CHEESE
2 CUP MACARONI (ELBOW PASTA)
1/2 CUP MILK
SALT & PEPPER

COOK ONION & MACARONI IN A SAUCEPAN OF WATER WITH A BIT OF SALT.
FOLLOW PACK INSTR-UCTIONS. SHOULD TAKE ABOUT 10 MIN.

DRAIN OFF WATER. PLACE MAC. & ONION BACK IN SAUCEPAN.
STIR CHEESE & MILK THRU THE MACARONI.

ADD A SPRINKLE OF SALT & PEPPER.
IF YOU'RE REALLY BRAVE, ADD A TBSP OF PARSLEY - HEAPS OF VITAMINS IN THAT!
13-00

Useful Tip

Turn the element or burner off before removing a pot or pan from the stovetop.

BACON & TOMATO
WAGON-WHEEL PASTA
SERVES 2
• 2 cups DRIED WAGON WHEEL PASTA (or macaroni)
• 1 TBSP BUTTER (or margarine)
• 4-6 BACON RASHERS
• 1 TBSP CHOPPED PARSLEY
• 1 LARGE TOMATO (cut up)

COOK PASTA IN BOILING SALTED WATER, FOLLOWING DIRECTIONS ON PACK.
How they 'spect a sausage dog to do that?!

DRAIN IN A SIEVE or COLANDER.
GLURGLE
SLOSH
Place butter or marg. in the pan the pasta was boiled in (no need to wash first).

ADD BACON & COOK 3-4 MIN. ADD PARSLEY & CUT-UP TOMATO.
COOL
MIX
TOGETHER WITH DRAINED PASTA & SERVE.
John Stringer 10-00

Useful Tip

Leaving the kitchen nice and tidy will make everyone happy and they'll be pleased to let you cook another time.

SWEET CORN FRITTERS
• 310 gm can of cream-style sweet corn
• 3/4 self-raising flour
• 1/4 milk
• 2 eggs (separate into yolks & whites)
• salt & pepper
• 50 gm. butter
• 3 tbsp oil
SERVES 4
IN A BOWL, MIX THE CORN, SELF-RAISING FLOUR, MILK, EGG YOLKS, SALT & PEPPER

IN A SEPARATE SMALL BOWL, BEAT THE EGG WHITES UNTIL STIFF.
Fold the egg whites into the mixture.

MELT 50 GM BUTTER & 3 TBSP OIL IN A NON-STICK PAN.
Cook spoonfuls of the mixture over a med. heat for 3 min.
DRAIN ON PAPER TOWELS.
SERVE WITH A GREEN SALAD OR WITH A DOLLOP OF SOUR CREAM OR TOMATO SAUCE.
11-00

Useful Tip

When melting butter in the microwave, leave the paper on it or cover the bowl with a paper towel or cling wrap to avoid butter splatters all over the inside of the oven.

BACON WRAPPED CHICKEN BREAST
• 1 SINGLE CHICKEN BREAST (boneless with skin on) PER PERSON
• 2 RASHERS RINDLESS STREAKY BACON, PER PERSON
LEAVE THE CHICKEN SKIN ON (the skin keeps the chicken moist & prevents it drying out).
CLUK
"All the breast"
SERVES 4

WRAP THE WHOLE THING UP IN THE 2 BACON RASHERS (like bandages).
SALT
PEPPER
Sprinkle with salt & pepper.
BAKE IN A HOT OVEN (200c) UNTIL BACON & CHICKEN ARE CRISP & COOKED THRU (about 30 min.)
Hot Dog!

Useful Tip

Wear an apron to keep your clothes clean.

25
BaBY
SAV-OURY
PIKELETS
• 1/2 tsp salt
• 1 tsp baking soda
• 1 milk
• 2 eggs
• 2 flour
• 2 tsp cream of tartar
• 1 tbsp finely chopped parsley
PLACE ALL INGREDIENTS IN A FOOD PROCESSOR OR BLENDER. MIX UNTIL SMOOTH & WELL-COMBINED.
MILK
THICK SAUSAGE DOG
ADD EXTRA MILK IF MIXTURE IS TOO THICK.
LADLE SPOONFULS INTO A NONSTICK PAN OVER MEDIUM HEAT.
You can use an electric frypan...
ZORK
For the first pikelet, you may need a tiny bit of greasing to the pan.
Tip: to achieve a lovely golden brown surface, don't grease the pan between batches.
COOK BOTH SIDES (approx. 2 min. each side) & COOL ON A RACK.
Serve buttered & sprinkled with grated cheese or spread with dip.
8.00

Useful Tip

To test an egg for freshness, place it in a bowl of water. A fresh egg will sink but a stale egg will float as it is lighter.

YUM
'FLOATIES' FOR TEA

EGGS
RULE 4
BREAKFAST
6 BREAD SLICES (TOAST THICK)
1/2 CHOPPED HAM OR LEAN BACON
1/2 GRATED
6 EGGS
1 1/4 MILK
SALT & PEPPER

SERVES 6
GREASE OR SPRAY WITH OIL A SQUARE CAKE TIN (APPROX. 20 CM SIZE) OR LASAGNE DISH.

TEAR OR CUT BREAD INTO BITE-SIZE PIECES & PLACE IN DISH.
SPRINKLE THE HAM, CHEESE, SALT & PEPPER OVER.

MIX EGGS & MILK THEN POUR OVER. ALLOW TO REST & SOAK UP EGGY MIX (ABOUT 15 MIN.)
TURN OVEN ON TO 180 C.
COOK FOR 30 MIN. UNTIL PUFFY & GOLDEN. COOL, THEN SLICE.
16·00

Useful Tip

Arrange the oven racks where you'll need them before you turn the oven on.

BANANA
GROOVY SMOOVIE
2 BANANAS
1 YOGHURT
1 MILK, lowfat is healthy
1 SCOOP of ICE-CREAM

PLACE EVERYTHING IN A BLENDER. FIT THE LID PROPERLY AND...
WHIZ
FOR 1 MIN.
TIME IT!
POUR INTO LONG GLASSES. DECORATE WITH A ON THE SIDE OF THE GLASS.
KLINK

Useful Tip

Never put your hands into a blender or try to scrape the sides with a spatula while the blender is still running.

SIMPLE
CAULIFLOWER
CHEESE
1 SMALL CAULI. broken into florets
1 GRATED CHEESE
1/2 SOUR CREAM, 150 gm
SALT & PEPPER
SERVES 4

COOK CAULI FLORETS IN BOILING SALTED WATER 6-8 MIN.
CHECK THEY'RE COOKED. DON'T LET 'EM GO TO MUSH.

DRAIN WATER OFF. PLACE CAULI FLORETS IN DISH (OR CAKE TIN) THAT CAN BE GRILLED.
PLASTIC DIDN'T WORK!

SLOSH SOUR CREAM OVER CAULI SPRINKLE WITH CHEESE, SALT & PEPPER.
PLACE UNDER HOT GRILL 3-4 MIN. UNTIL CHEESE BUBBLES & BROWNS.

Useful
Tip

Turn saucepan handles to the side so you don't knock them off the stovetop and on to someone else.

GORK!
SP-TANG

COLESLAW FOR ALL THE CREW
SERVES 6

INGREDIENTS
1 HARD CABBAGE
1 RED EATING APPLE
2 BIG CARROTS
2 STICKS CELERY
1/2 SULTANAS
6 TBSP MAYONNAISE
6 TBSP YOGHURT (PLAIN or NATURAL).

FINELY SLICE THE CABBAGE (USE A FOOD PROCESSOR IF IT HAS A SHREDD -ING BLADE).
CHOPu.
CORE & GRATE APPLE (LEAVE SKIN ON).
PEEL & GRATE CARROTS. SLICE CELERY FINELY. MIX EVERYTHING TOGETHER. NYUM.
Hot Dog!
SEASON TO TASTE WITH SALT & PEPPER
17.00

Useful Tip

Hold the knife firmly and handle it with care – don't fool around with knives.

Rice Bubble
MARSHMALLOW
BARS
• 100 GM BUTTER or MARGARINE
• 1 PACKET (300 gm) MARSHMALLOWS
• 4 RICE BUBBLES
• 1/2 CHOC CHIPS

MELT MARSHIES & BUTTER IN A LARGE PAN OVER MEDIUM HEAT UNTIL SMOOTH.

ADD RICE BUBBLES & CHOCOLATE CHIPS.
MIX WELL
RICE BUB
TIP INTO A GREASED OR OIL-SPRAYED CAKE TIN.

WET YOUR HANDS WITH COLD WATER. PRESS MIXTURE FLAT
CHILL IN FRIDGE THEN CUT INTO PIECES.
22.00

Useful Tip

Make sure pot and pan handles are not over another element or burner as the handle will heat up and give you a bad burn when you try to pick it up.

FABULOUS FUDGE
WITH NUTS & BOLTS
500 GM ICING SUGAR
1/2 CUP COCOA
1/2 CUP MILK POWDER
125 GM BUTTER
1/2 CUP WATER
1/2 CUP CHOPPED NUTS or SULTANAS

LINE A CAKE TIN (Approx. 20 X 20 CM) WITH TIN FOIL.
HEAT THE MILK POWDER, BUTTER & WATER TILL BOILING (OR MICROWAVE).

STIR ICING SUGAR, COCOA, SULTANAS INTO HOT MIX 'TIL SMOOTH. POUR INTO TIN.
ADD NUTS & SUL-TAN-AS.
CUT WHEN COLD & FIRM.
E2P2 LEMON SQUEEZY!

Useful Tip

Always ask an adult's permission before cooking.

APPLE & GRAPE SALAD
2 APPLES & 30 FRESH GRAPES (Red or Green)
1 LOW FAT YOGHURT
3 TBSP SOUR CREAM
2 TBSP SQEEZY LIQUID HONEY

PLACE GRAPES IN FREEZER FOR 30 MIN. TO GET REALLY COLD. Brrr!

SLICE APPLES, REMOVE CORE BUT LEAVE SKIN ON.
SLICE
Yoghurt
HONE
MIX YOGHURT, SOUR CREAM & HONEY. MIX EVERYTHING TOGETHER

SERVE CHILLED WITH A SPRINKLE OF CHOPPED PARSLEY.
20.00

Useful Tip

Clean up as you cook – it makes less work at the end.

CHEESEY BREAD & BUTTERCUPS
12 SLICES SANDWICH BREAD (spread with butter or margarine)
1 GRATED CHEESE
3 MEDIUM TOMATOES
3 TBSP CHOPPED PARSLEY

PREHEAT OVEN TO 180 C.
CUT OFF CRUSTS. PRESS BREAD SLICES INTO MUFFIN TRAYS, BUTTER-SIDE DOWN.

BAKE FOR 15 MIN.
DIVIDE CHEESE AMONG CUPS. TOP WITH SLICED TOMATO, PARSLEY, SALT & PEPPER.

BAKE FOR 10 MIN. MORE UNTIL BREAD IS GOLDEN & CHEESE IS BUBBLY & MELTED.
CRUNCH
Hot Dog!
21.00
COOL BEFORE EATING.

Useful Tip

When opening the oven door, stand back so that the hot steam can escape before you try to remove anything. If you wear glasses, be careful as your glasses may fog up.

20
PUFFBALLS
125 GM GRATED CHEESE
3 TBSP BUTTER or MARGARINE
3/4 ☕ FLOUR
1/2 TSP BAKING POWDER
1/4 TSP SALT

PreHeat Oven to 200°c
IN A BOWL, MIX THE BUTTER & CHEESE INTO THE DRY INGREDIENTS UNTIL EVERYTHING IS BLENDED.
THIS COULD BE DONE IN A FOOD PROCESSOR.
ADD A FEW DROPS OF WATER TO CREATE A DOUGH.
SHAPE DOUGH INTO SMALL MARBLE-SIZE BALLS & PLACE ON A BAKING TRAY (an edged tray will stop them running off).
BAKE FOR 12-15 MIN. UNTIL GOLDEN BROWN.
23·00

Useful Tip

Wash your hands before preparing food but also dry them.

CHUNKY CHICKEN DIPPERS
1 DRY BREAD CRUMBS
4 MEDIUM CHICKEN BREASTS (No skin or bone)
1 EGG, 1 TBSP MILK
1 SMASHED CHEESEY CRACKER CRUMBS

CUT CHICKEN INTO LONG FINGER STRIPS.
HOW FOWL!

MIX THE BREAD & CRACKER CRUMBS IN A PLASTIC BAG. BEAT TOGETHER THE EGG & MILK.

DROP CHICKEN INTO EGG MIX, THEN PLACE IN PLASTIC BAG.
HOLD BAG CLOSED &
Shake

PLACE CHICKEN PIECES ON OVEN TRAY. SPRAY WITH OIL & BAKE AT 200C (15-20 MIN.) UNTIL GOLDEN CRISPY.

Useful Tip

Always check that you've turned off the oven or gas at the end of cooking.

WE'RE ALL GOIN' ON A LOOONNG SUMMER HOLIDAY
EZPZ CK

B.B.Q.
BANANA
SUNDAES
MAKES 4
4 PEELED BANANAS
4 TSP BUTTER or MARGARINE
4 TSP HONEY
VANILLA ICE-CREAM
YOU SCREAM, I'LL SCREAM, ALL SCREAM FOR ICE-CREAM

ON A SHEET OF TIN FOIL, PLACE A BANANA, TSP BUTTER & TSP HONEY. DO THIS 4 TIMES.
SERVES FOUR
HON
MARG
WRAP EACH SHEET OF FOIL INTO A SECURE PARCEL.
PLACE ON BBQ & COOK 5-6 MIN.

OPEN FOIL & TIP OVER A BOWL OF VANILLA ICE-CREAM.
Dig in!
CAREFUL, IT'S HOT & STEAMY WHEN OPENING PACKAGE.
26-01

Useful
Tip

To make a delicious caramel fudgy sauce, boil a can of sweetened condensed milk – take off the label, cover the can with water and gently boil with the lid on for 2–3 hours. Wait till it cools before opening the can.

MICROWAVED
SCRAMBLED
EGGS
WITH CHEESE
BUTTER or MARG.
4 EGGS.
HANDFUL of
GRATED CHEESE
1 TBSP PARSLEY
SALT & PEPPER
SERVES 4

MELT 1 TSP BUTTER OR MARGARINE IN A MICROWAVE BOWL.
ADD 4 EGGS. WHISK UNTIL FROTHY.

COOK ON HIGH 1 1/2 MIN. UNTIL JUST FIRM.
STIR 2 X DURING COOKING.

ADD GRATED CHEESE, CHOPPED PARSLEY, SALT & PEPPER.
STIR, THEN SIT FOR 1 MIN. SERVE OVER TOAST. YUM!
25-01

Useful Tip

Be careful not to burn yourself. Even though microwaves go right through containers without heating them, the hot food inside can make the container hot.

SPEEDIE CUSTARD!!

INGREDIENTS
- 1/4 ☕ CUSTARD POWDER
- 2 TBSP SUGAR
- 2 ☕ MILK

NOW THAT'S FAST FOOD.

IN A LARGE MICROWAVE BOWL OR JUG, WHISK 1/4 ☕ CUSTARD POWDER WITH THE SUGAR & 1/2 ☕ MILK UNTIL SMOOTHLY MIXED.

ADD ANOTHER 1 1/2 ☕ MILK & MICROWAVE ON HIGH FOR 6 MIN.

6 MIN

MMMMMMMMMMM

STIR 3 TIMES DURING COOKING (i.e. EVERY 2 MIN.)

EzPz LEMON SQUEEZY

THE CUSTARD SHOULD BE THICK & SMOOTH. (A WIRE WHISK IS BEST FOR STIRRING).

John Turner 24.00

Spills should be cleaned up immediately, especially on the floor, to avoid anyone skidding or slipping over.

5 MINUTE
CHILLI
BEANS
500 GM LEAN MINCEMEAT
1 CAN CHILLI or KIDNEY BEANS
1/2 TOMATO-PASTA SAUCE
HOT DOG!

IN A LARGE NON-STICK FRYPAN, ADD 1 TBSP OIL. COOK MINCEMEAT, STIRRING FOR 4-5 MIN. UNTIL NO LONGER PINK.

PASTA SAUCE
ADD CHILLI BEANS & PASTA SAUCE, SALT & PEPPER TO TASTE.

IF YOU LIKE IT
Hot
ADD CHILLI POWDER OR PEPPER SAUCE - BUT JUST A SMIDGE.
EAT AS IS OR ROLL UP IN A TORTILLA WITH CHOPPED LETTUCE & GRATED CHEESE.
27.01

Useful Tip

Keep long hair tied back and roll up your sleeves before you start preparing food.

TOMATO & BASIL PASTA SAUCE

Serves 4

3 LARGE TOMATOES
2 ☕ PASTA
1/4 ☕ BASIL PESTO SAUCE
TSP CRUSHED GARLIC

CHOP UP THE TOMATOES, ADD BASIL PESTO SAUCE AND THE CRUSHED GARLIC.

COOK PASTA (2 CUPS MACARONI) IN SALTED WATER TIL TENDER

TOSS THE MIXTURE WITH THE DRAINED COOKED PASTA IN A LARGE SERVING BOWL.

'TOSS' DOESN'T MEAN THROW IT IN THE AIR!

SERVE IMMEDIATELY WITH FRESHLY GROUND PEPPER TO TASTE.

28-01

Ask an adult to drain foods cooked in lots of water, such as pasta. Pans full of water are heavy and wobble a lot. If not done right the water and the steam could burn you.

Easy Peasy Lemon Squeezy

HONEY GARLIC GLAZED CARROTS
4-6 LARGE CARROTS CUT INTO THIN DISKS or SLICES
2 TBSP LIQUID HONEY
2 TSP CRUSHED GARLIC
1 TBSP OIL.

IN A LARGE NON-STICK PAN, TOSS CARROTS, OIL & GARLIC.
THEN ADD 3/4 WATER. BRING TO BOIL.

ADD HONEY. SIMMER 7-10 MIN. UNTIL CARROTS ARE TENDER & SOFT & MOST OF THE WATER HAS EVAPORATED.
Yo, Hot Dog! People say carrots help you see in the dark...
Lettuce eat heaps of 'em
SERVE WITH A SPRINKLING OF PARSLEY, SALT & PEPPER TO TASTE.
29-01

Useful Tip

Don't hold things and cut them – put them down on a chopping board. Always cut with the blade of the knife pointing away from you.

CHOCOLATE MOUSSE CUPCAKES
250 GM MILK CHOCOLATE
3 EGGS
1/4 FLOUR
ARE YOU A MAN, MOUSSE OR MOOSE?

PREHEAT OVEN TO 180°C
MELT CHOCOLATE IN A MICROWAVE BOWL ON MEDIUM, STIRRING OFTEN
Hot Dog
WHISK IN EGGS & FLOUR

PLACE 6 CUPCAKE PAPER LINERS INTO MUFFIN TINS & SPOON IN THE MIXTURE.
BAKE 12-15 MIN. UNTIL SIDES SET BUT CENTRES ARE STILL LIQUID.
COOL 2-3 MIN. CAREFULLY PEEL-OFF PAPERS (THE CENTRES WILL BE A WARM MOUSSE CONSISTENCY).
SERVE WITH WHIPPED CREAM & SHAVED CHOC.
30-01

Useful Tip

Melt chocolate on medium or medium-low in short 30-second bursts in the microwave rather than in a pot on the stove.

SESAME
CHICKPEA
NIBBLES
ROOKY COOK
2 [cup] COOKED CANNED CHICKPEAS (DRAINED)
1 TBSP ASIAN SESAME OIL
1 TSP GARLIC SALT
NIBBLE NIBBLE
HOT DOG

HEAT A NON-STICK PAN. ADD CHICKPEAS, COOK OVER MED. HEAT FOR 2 MIN. STIRRING CONSTANTLY.
CHICKPEAS SHOULD GO GOLDEN & DRY.
ADD SESAME OIL & GARLIC SALT. STIR TO COAT WELL.
1 TBSP
OIL
EAT WHEN COOL.
Hot Dog, to clean the kitchen floor, should we mop-it or muppet?
31-01

Useful Tip

Never use wet hands to switch on or plug in anything electrical.

EZPZ
FOR THE WHOLE FAMILY
MEXICAN
MEAT-LOAF
EEZ REELY GOOD, 'OMBRE

•750 GM MINCED MEAT
•250 GM SAUSAGE MEAT
•1 FRESH BREAD CRUMBS MIXED WITH SALT & PEPPER
•1 1/2 THICK SPICY SALSA or PASTA SAUCE (Med or Hot).

WEAR PLASTIC GLOVES & USE HANDS TO MUSH EVERYTHING TOGETHER.
TAKE A 6 CAPACITY LOAF TIN.
GREASE TIN & LINE WITH BAKING PAPER (or TIN FOIL). PRESS MIXTURE IN. BAKE 180 C FOR ABOUT 1 HOUR.
SERVE WITH TOMATO SAUCE.
34-01

Useful Tip

Lining baking tin bases with non-stick baking paper makes removing a loaf or cake so much easier.

MARMALADE CHICKEN

FOWL FOOD?

SERVES FOUR

1/2 cup ORANGE MARMALADE
2 TBSP SOY SAUCE
4 CHICKEN PORTIONS (Legs, breasts, etc)

MIX MARMALADE & SOY SAUCE.

SPOON OVER CHICKEN TO COAT WELL.

TURN & CHECK CHICKEN IS PROPERLY COOKED RIGHT THROUGH.

COOK APPROX. 30-40 MIN. IN AN OVEN AT 200 C.

Don't forget ...

Useful
Tip

Use a kitchen timer so you don't forget the food in the oven!

WE'RE ALL GOIN' ON A LOOOONG SUMMER HOLIDAY
EZPZ CK

GOOD FOR THE SOUL AND JUST LIKE MOTHER USED TO MAKE.
Lemon
CHICKEN
SOUP
4 CHICKEN STOCK
1/2 LONG-GRAIN RICE
1 JUICY LEMON

HEAT CHICKEN STOCK. ADD RICE, GENTLY BOIL 12 MIN.
Hot Dog!

ADD GRATED LEMON RIND & SQUEEZED JUICE (REMOVE PIPS) INTO SOUP & STIR.

ADD SALT & PEPPER TO TASTE. SERVE WITH CRUSTY BREAD.
Z
32-01

Useful
Tip

Half a cup of uncooked rice will give one cup of cooked rice.

ParMEsan cheese & NUT wafers
THIS IS CRAZY
Nuts? Nuts? Did Someone Say Nuts?
1 [cup] GRATED PARMESAN CHEESE
2 TBSP CHOPPED NUTS

Makes 8-10
ON A SHEET OF BAKING PAPER PLACED ON A BAKING TRAY, SPRINKLE SMALL CIRCLES OF PARMESAN [cheese] (about the width of a glass). SPRINKLE NUTS OVER.

COOK 180 C 8-10 MIN UNTIL [cheese] IS ALL MELTED & GOLDEN.
COOL FOR 2 MIN ON THE PAPER, THEN PEEL OFF & COOL ON WIRE RACK
37-01

Useful Tip

Store nuts in plastic bags in the freezer. They are high in oils and tend to go rancid and 'off' if stored in the pantry.

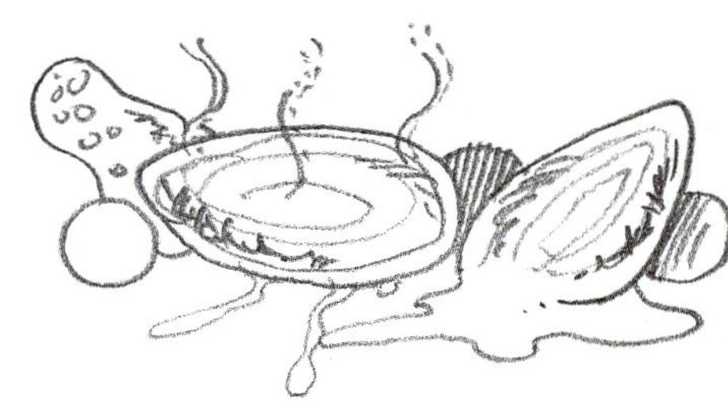

GREEK
SPINACH
SALAD

4 HANDFULS WASHED SPINACH LEAVES (i.e. no grit or snails)

100 GM FETA CHEESE (cut or cubed)

1 ☕ OLIVES

1/2 ☕ CREAMY GARLIC SALAD DRESSING

TΦSS ΛLTΘGΣTHΣR. KΣΣP KHILLΣD BΣFΦRΣ SΣRVING. SPRINKLΣ WITH KHΦPPΣD PΛRSLΣΨ, SΛLT & PΣPPER.

Useful
Tip

Always dress a salad just before serving. If left too long with dressing on, leaves will go limp and soggy.

Classic Pasta Alfredo
SERVES IV
4 cooked drained pasta
50 GM BUTTER/MARG.
1/2 CREAM
1/2 GRATED PARMESAN CHEESE
PARSLEY & PEPPER

MIX 'N' MELT CREAM, BUTTER & CHEESE IN A HOT SAUCEPAN.

ADD DRAINED PASTA & LOTS OF VITAMIN-PACKED PARSLEY & GROUND PEPPER.

TOSS & SERVE IMMEDIATELY.

Useful Tip

Get an adult to supervise or to be on hand to help with tricky tasks.

CHEWY COCONUT MACAROONS
Psst! Ya heard tha' teel o' tha' wild MacarOOOOn beastie, laddie?
...the one where it does its scone?
1 BEAT EGG WHITES STIFF IN A BOWL.
2 MIX THE COCONUT & CONDENSED MILK.
3 MIX 1 & 2 & SPOON ONTO A BAKING PAPER-LINED OVEN TRAY.

4 BAKE AT 180 C 20 MIN. UNTIL GOLDEN BROWN ON TOP & WELL-BROWNED ON THE BOTTOM.
5 COOL 5 MIN. ON TRAY, THEN COOL ON A WIRE RACK.
LEMME SEE

MAKES 30 COOKIES
4 COCONUT
1 (396 gm) SWEETENED CONDENSED MILK
BONK
3 EGG WHITES

Useful Tip

Always preheat the oven before putting food in to cook.

Easy Peasy Lemon Squeezy

LEMON BUTTER
MAKES 2 SMALL JARS
50 GM BUTTER
3 EGGS
1 SUGAR
1/2 JUICE (finely grated lemon rind & juice of 2 lemons)

MELT THE BUTTER IN A MEDIUM to LARGE MICROWAVE-PROOF JUG or BOWL.
WHISK IN OTHER INGREDIENTS ON HIGH FOR 1 MIN.

WHISK AGAIN & MICRO-WAVE IN BURSTS OF 30 SEC. WHISKING EACH TIME UNTIL LEMON IS THICK & GLOSSY.
IT SHOULD TAKE ONLY 4-5 MIN.
Whisk Whisk
!
SUCK SUCK
POUR INTO HOT STERILISED JARS

Useful Tip

Heating a lemon in the microwave for about 20 seconds on high will make it easier to squeeze and will produce more juice.

Red & Green Salad
4 (OR HANDFULS) OF TORN MIXED GREEN SALAD LEAVES
SERVES 4 HUNGRY SALAD LOVERS
1/2 PREPARED SALAD DRESSING OR VINAIGRETTE
CHOPPED
2 MIXED GREENS (CUCUMBER, GREEN PEPPER, PARSLEY, CELERY, CHIVES, etc)
2 MIXED REDS (RED PEPPER, RED APPLE, RED ONION, CHERRY TOMATOES, etc)
FEELIN' A BIT BLUE!
I SEE RED!
I'M BROWNED OFF, ACTUALLY

TOSS EVERYTHING TOGETHER IN A LARGE BOWL. DRIZZLE DRESSING OVER.
TOSS TOSS
I'LL BE MOTHER
ERG
SERVE IMMEDIATELY
SPLAT

Useful Tip

To wash greens such as lettuce or spinach leaves, cover with water in the sink and sprinkle with salt. This will make any bugs, slugs or snails rise to the top (yum!).

Baked Crispy Potato Fritters
12
2 LARGE POTATOES (Peeled)
50 GM MELTED BUTTER
1/2 TSP SALT, PINCH O' PEPPER

BOIL POTATOES FOR EXACTLY 10 MIN. UNTIL JUST GETTING SOFT. DRAIN & COOL.
PEEL
PEEL
PEEL
SPUDS
TURN OVEN TO 180 C. GRATE COOL POTATO & MIX WITH MELTED BUTTER, SALT & PEPPER.
SPOON INTO A 12-HOLE MUFFIN TRAY. COOK 30-35 MIN. UNTIL CRISP & GOLDEN
CAREFULLY TIP OUT ONTO PAPER TOWELS TO COOL A BIT. EAT WARM.
Hot Warm Dog
FRITTERS CAN BE REHEATED
41.01

Useful Tip

Butter has measurement guides on the paper wrap.

HEAVE
HEAVE
1000 MILES
BUTTER

EZPZ PAVLOVA
3 EGG WHITES[1]
1 CASTER SUGAR
1 TSP VANILLA ESSENCE
1 TBSP CORNFLOUR
1 TBSP VINEGAR (Malt or White)
Ta lofa lava! Love a 'lova!
1. KEEP THE YOLKS FOR ANOTHER RECIPE, LIKE SCRAMBLED EGGS.

HEAT OVEN TO 120 C (very low). BEAT EGG WHITES IN A NON-PLASTIC BOWL UNTIL STIFF.
SLOWLY (1 TSP AT A TIME) ADD SUGAR & KEEP BEATING (an electric beater is ideal).

THE MIXTURE GETS THICK, GLOSSY & PURE WHITE. ADD VANILLA, CORN-FLOUR & VINEGAR. MIX WELL.
PLOP ONTO A BAKING PAPER-LINED TRAY. DON'T SPREAD OUT TOO THIN. SMOOTH INTO A FLAT ROUND SHAPE.
COOK 1 HR, THEN COOL ON TRAY. COVER WITH WHIPPED CREAM, FRUIT & CHOC. CHIPS.[2]
[2]DICED KIWIFRUIT IS A NZ SPECIALTY.
42-01

Useful Tip

Don't keep opening and closing or banging the oven door while a pavlova is cooking.

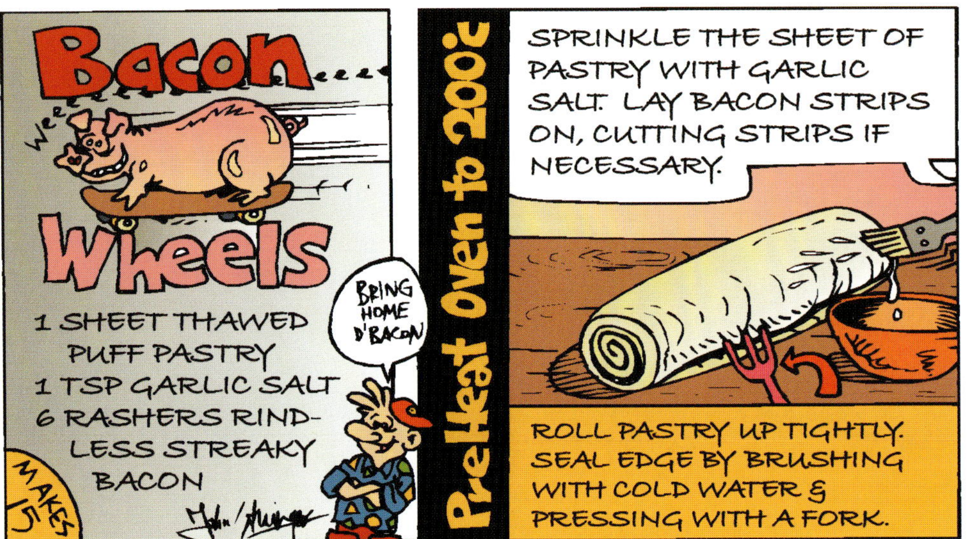
Bacon.....
Weeee
Wheels
1 SHEET THAWED PUFF PASTRY
1 TSP GARLIC SALT
6 RASHERS RINDLESS STREAKY BACON
MAKES 15
BRING HOME D'BACON
PreHeat Oven to 200c
SPRINKLE THE SHEET OF PASTRY WITH GARLIC SALT. LAY BACON STRIPS ON, CUTTING STRIPS IF NECESSARY.
ROLL PASTRY UP TIGHTLY. SEAL EDGE BY BRUSHING WITH COLD WATER & PRESSING WITH A FORK.

SLICE INTO 15 DISCS (size of a 50c piece) & LAY ON A GREASED BAKING TRAY.

COOK 10-15 MIN., TURN & COOK 5 MIN. MORE UNTIL PUFFED & GOLDEN.

EAT WARM -YUM!! 43-01

Useful Tip

Wash knives and sharp tools individually. If you put them in a sink full of soapy water, you or someone else could reach in and grab a blade or sharp edge by mistake.

AARGGH TOMATO SAUCE -NOT!

Chocolate
FUDGE
Brownies
1/4 COCOA
1 SUGAR
2 EGGS
125 GM BUTTER (Melted)
1 TSP VANILLA ESSENCE
1 FLOUR
1 TSP BAKING POWDER
(OPTIONAL) 1/2 CHOPPED WALNUTS OR ALMONDS
PreHeat oven to 180°C

MIX BUTTER, COCOA, SUGAR, EGGS & VANILLA. STIR IN FLOUR, BAKING POWDER & OPTIONAL NUTS.
POUR INTO 20 CM SQUARE TIN LINED WITH BAKING PAPER.

COOK 30 MIN. (IT MIGHT SINK A BIT IN THE MIDDLE). COOL ON A WIRE RACK.
DUST WITH ICING SUGAR WHEN COLD & CUT INTO FINGERS OR BLOCKS.
44-01

Useful Tip

To dust with icing sugar, put icing sugar into a flour sifter and shake it gently over the brownies.

Garlic Jacket Wedges (For 4 Hungry KiDS)
4 LARGE POTATOES (SCRUBBED)
3 TBSP OLIVE OIL
1 TSP GARLIC SALT
1
2
3, 4

TURN OVEN TO 220 C.
CUT POTATOES LENGTHWAYS IN HALF, THEN IN HALF AGAIN, THEN INTO WEDGES.
Chop!
PLACE ON AN OVEN TRAY, DRIZZLE WITH OIL.

SPRINKLE WITH GARLIC SALT. BAKE UNTIL CRISPY & GOLDEN. SERVE WITH DIPS OR SOUR CREAM.
NYUM!
Hot Dog!

'Floury' potatoes are best for wedges, chips, roasting and mashing; don't use 'waxy' or new potatoes – they're best for salads.

FOR 6
MANDARIN & CHOCOLATE MARSHMALLOW SUNDAE
Gives MING zing

3 CHOPPED CHOCOLATE or CHOC. CHIPS
1 CREAM
VANILLA & CHOC. ICE-CREAM
1 PACKET MARSHMALLOWS
6 MANDARINS or A CAN OF MANDARIN SEGMENTS

MELT THE CHOCOLATE & CREAM TOGETHER IN A SMALL SAUCEPAN (OR MICROWAVE IT).
STIR UNTIL SMOOTHLY COMBINED.
SCOOP THE VANILLA CHOC. ICE-CREAM INTO GLASSES. SPRINKLE WITH MARSHMALLOWS & MANDARIN SEGMENTS.
YOU CAN USE FRUIT OTHER THAN MANDARINS.
POUR THE CHOC. FUDGE OVER.

Useful Tip

Before scooping out ice cream, dip the scoop into a jug of hot water to warm it, then the ice cream will scoop easily!

ice-cream

BAKED
PANCAKE
2 EGGS
2 TBSP SUGAR
1/2 MILK
1/2 FLOUR
50 GM BUTTER
serves 4

BEAT EGGS, SUGAR, MILK & FLOUR IN A BLENDER OR PROCESSOR.
RARGGGG
clik
PUT BUTTER IN A CAKE TIN OR SMALL LASAGNE TYPE DISH (20 X 20CM).

MELT IN OVEN AT 220 C.
POUR PANCAKE MIX ONTO THE MELTED BUTTER & COOK 15 MIN. UNTIL PUFFED UP.

SERVE WITH LEMON JUICE & SUGAR OR FRUIT & ICE-CREAM.

Useful Tip

Make sure the blender lid is on properly – blenders with the lid off act like geysers!

CURRIED
ChickPeA
NacHos
LOOK, NACH-NOSE!
SERVES

1 LARGE BAG O' CORN CHIPS
2 GRATED CHEESE
1 DRAINED CHICKPEAS (approx. 2)
1 'READY to HEAT' CURRY SAUCE (ie pasta sauce)
SOUR CREAM
HERBS to SERVE.

DIVIDE CORN CHIPS BETWEEN 4 PLATES.
SPRINKLE WITH CHEESE.
MIX DRAINED CHICKPEAS WITH CURRY SAUCE & SPOON ONTO CORN CHIPS. MICRO-WAVE EACH PLATE TO WARM CHIPS & MELT CHEESE (1 MIN. EACH).
ISN'T CHICK PEE FOWL?
SERVE WITH DOLLOP OF SOUR CREAM. SPRINKLE WITH PARSLEY OR CORIANDER.
50-01

Useful Tip

Being tidy and neat can prevent accidents – wash dirty tools as you finish with them and wipe up spills immediately.

CREAMY
PUMPKIN
3 PEELED PUMPKIN (CUT INTO CUBES)
3 WATER
1 MILK or CREAM
1 TSP CINNAMON
SALT & PEPPER
PARSLEY TO SERVE
SOUP

PLACE PUMPKIN & WATER IN A MEDIUM SAUCEPAN. BRING TO BOIL & COOK APPROX. 20 MIN. (UNTIL SOFT & MUSHY).
BLOP
BLOOP
SERVES 4
TRANSFER TO A FOOD PRO-CESSOR (OR BLENDER). ADD CINNAMON & MILK.

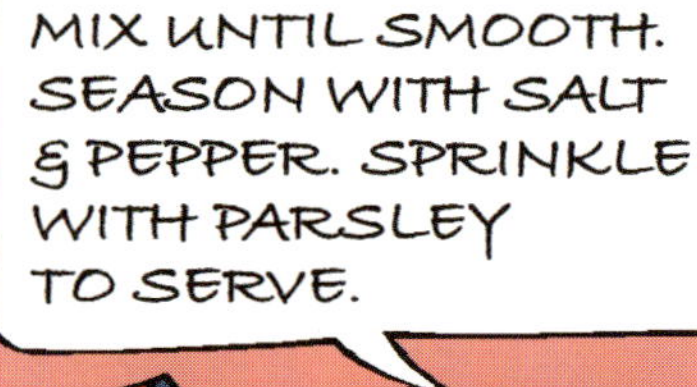
MIX UNTIL SMOOTH. SEASON WITH SALT & PEPPER. SPRINKLE WITH PARSLEY TO SERVE.

Useful Tip

Soak dirty dishes (but not sharp knives) in a sink of soapy water to loosen baked-on grime.

BANANA
CHOC
CHiP
MUFFiNS
1 BANANA (RIPE & MASHED WITH A FORK)
1+1/2 SELF-RAISING FLOUR. 3/4 MILK
3/4 SUGAR,
1/2 CHOC. CHIPS
1 EGG, 1/4 OIL
MAKES NINE

PreHeaT OVeN to 180c
MIX MIX MIX MIX
MIX ALL INGREDIENTS. DON'T OVER MIX, JUST COMBINE.

SPOON INTO A WELL-GREASED MUFFIN TRAY. COOK FOR 20 MIN. COOL ON A WIRE RACK.

DROOOL

Useful Tip

Always ice or frost cup cakes, cakes or muffins when they are cold or the icing will run straight off.

I'M OUTTA HERE
TOO HOT FOR ME TO HANDLE

APPLE CRUMBLE

SIX APPLES

PEELED, SLICED & COOKED WITH 1/2 CUP WATER UNTIL SOFT

100 GM BUTTER

1/2 TSP CINNAMON

3/4 CUP BROWN SUGAR

3/4 CUP FLOUR

SERVES 4

IN A FOOD PROCESSOR MIX BUTTER, CINNAMON, SUGAR & FLOUR.

SPRINKLE THE MIX OVER THE STEWED APPLE IN A PIE DI.H

BAKE AT 180 C FOR 40 MIN.

SERVE HOT WITH ICE-CREAM OR WHIPPED CREAM.

DON'T LET THAT TUMMY RUMBLE. FILL IT WITH APPLE CRUMBLE.

Turn off the mixer or processor before reaching into the mixing bowl. Never reach in with your hands or try to scrape the sides of the bowl with a spatula while the mixer is still running.

BUTTERSCOTCH SAUCE
WHAT YE RECKON LADDIE? IS'T TH' SCOTS IN TH' BLUD OR TH' SCOTCH IN TH' BLUD?
MAKES 2
100 GM BUTTER
1 BROWN SUGAR
1 TBSP CORNFLOUR
1/4 WATER, 3/4 CREAM

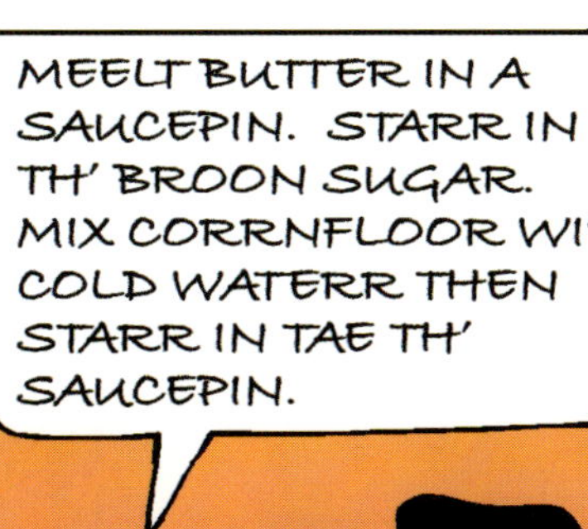
MEELT BUTTER IN A SAUCEPIN. STARR IN TH' BROON SUGAR. MIX CORRNFLOOR WI' COLD WATERR THEN STARR IN TAE TH' SAUCEPIN.

ADD CREAM (NOT TAE IRISH CREAM) UND SIMMERR.
KEEP STARRING UNTE TH' MIX THICKENS AN' STARRTS TAE BUBBLE.

SERVE O'ER YE FAV-OORITE ICE-CREAM - THE BAIRNS 'LL LOVE 'E FOR IT!
OCH AYE!

Useful Tip

Make sure the stovetop is clear of tea towels, mitts and cookbooks.

Breakfast Eggs 'N' Muffin
IS THAT LIKE SLOW LUNCH?
1 ENGLISH-STYLE MUFFIN
1 SMALL EGG
1 SLICE HAM (OR SOME SHAVED HAM)
2 TBSP GRATED CHEESE

SPLIT MUFFIN IN HALF & SCOOP-OUT A NEST HOLE FOR THE EGG. (NOW TOAST MUFFIN IF YOU LIKE). BREAK EGG CAREFULLY INTO HOLE & PIERCE YOLK A FEW TIMES.

LAY THE HAM OVER THE TOP & SPRINKLE WITH GRATED CHEESE. PLACE ON A PLATE & COVER WITH A PAPER TOWEL. MICROWAVE FOR 1 MIN. ON HIGH.

YUMSVILLE
CHECK EGG IS COOKING. 'MIGHT NEED LONGER.

Useful Tip

Don't overbeat or use a food processor for muffins. Just lightly moisten the dry ingredient by gently mixing. This produces light, smooth-topped muffins.

NAUGHTY MUFFINS!
WHIP
WHIP
THWACK

MICROWAVE APRICOT JAM PUDDIES in a CUP
YOU CAN USE OTHER FLAVOURS
4 TBSP APRICOT JAM
50 GM BUTTER or MARGARINE (MELTED)
SERVES 4
SPRAY OR GREASE 4 COFFEE MUGS. PUT 1 TBSP OF JAM IN THE BOTTOM OF EACH CUP. MIX BUTTER, EGG & SUGAR IN A BOWL. ADD FLOUR, BAKING POWDER & MILK. MIX TILL SMOOTH.
SCRUNCH
MUNCH
CRUNCH
1/4 SUGAR
1 FLOUR, 1 EGG
1 TSP BAKNG POWDER, 1/2 MILK

SPOON MIXTURE INTO 4 MUGS. PLACE MUGS IN MICROWAVE, COOK TOGETHER, APPROX. 4 MIN. (ON HIGH).
LET THEM STAND FOR 2 MIN. RUN A KNIFE 'ROUND EDGES, TIP OUT.

Useful Tip

1 teaspoon = 5 ml

1 tablespoon = 5 ml

3 teaspoons = 1 tablespoon

4 tablespoons = 1/4 cup

1 cup = 250ml

Microwave Mixed BERRY Jam
MAKES 2 JARS
MIXE
ERRY
500 GM MIXED BERRIES (STRAW/BLACK or RASP/BERRIES, FROZEN or FRESH)
1/4 LEMON JUICE
2 SUGAR
I'M INA JAM!

PLACE BERRIES IN A DEEP BOWL. COVER. COOK ON HIGH 4 MIN. MASH THE BERRIES. (CAREFUL, IT'S HOT!)
MASH
SQUEEACH
MASH
ADD THE LEMON JUICE & SUGAR & STIR WELL.
COOK ON HIGH 20 MIN. STIR EVERY 4 MIN. OR SO. ALLOW TO REST 5 MIN. THEN POUR INTO HOT STERILISED JARS.
BERRY GOOD
COVER & LABEL WHEN COOLED.
55-01

Useful Tip

Heating clean jars in the oven at 140°C for 15 minutes will sterilise them.

HOT CHEESE SAUCE
TO GO OVER VEGES
MAKES 2
50 GM BUTTER
1/4 FLOUR
2 MILK
1 GRATED
CHEESE
SALT & PEPPER

MELT BUTTER IN MICROWAVE. COVER WITH A PAPER TOWEL TO AVOID SPLATTERS.
BEEP BEEP
0:30
COOK ON HIGH FOR 2 MIN. WHISK AGAIN, NOW ADD CHEESE, SALT & PEPPER TO TASTE.
STIR IN FLOUR & ADD MILK. WHISK WELL TO AVOID LUMPS.
COOK ANOTHER 2 MIN. STIR WELL & POUR OVER HOT CRUNCHY VEGETABLES.

Useful Tip

Keep a bag of grated cheese in the freezer. It stops the cheese going mouldy and you can use it from frozen. It's also easier to sprinkle.

Short Bread
Biscuits
MAKES 30
250GM SOFTENED BUTTER (NOT MELTED)
3/4 ICING SUGAR
1/2 CORNFLOUR
1+1/2 FLOUR
HEY, SHORTY! WHERE'S THE BREAD?

BEAT BUTTER & ICING SUGAR TOGETHER. ADD CORNFLOUR & FLOUR.
FLOUR POWER
ON A FLOURED SURFACE, ROLL OUT UNTIL 1CM THICK.
CUT INTO SHAPES OR FINGERS & PLACE ON A GREASED TRAY. PRICK WITH A FORK.
BAKE AT 150 C 25-30 MIN. UNTIL PALE & GOLDEN.
COOL ON A WIRE RACK.
53-01

Useful Tip

If you don't have a rolling pin, a milk bottle makes a good substitute.

APRICOT RAISIN PORRIDGE
serves one
1/4 cup PORRIDGE OATS (ROLLED OATS)
1/2 cup MILK
1-2 TBSP RAISINS
2 DRIED APRICOTS (CUT UP)

MIX OATS, MILK, RAISINS & APRICOTS. MICROWAVE ON HIGH 1 MIN. STIR WELL.
MICROWAVE FOR A FURTHER 2 MIN., STIRRING UNTIL THICK & CREAMY. SERVE WITH MILK & BROWN SUGAR.
A QUICK BREAKFAST IDEA!
BUS STOP
58-01

Useful Tip

Check that machines are switched off before you turn on the power at the wall.

Glossary

Bake: To cook with hot, dry air. This is done in the oven.

Baking Powder & Baking Soda: Rising agents used to makes dough rise during baking. Can be acid, like cream of tartar, or alkali, like bicarbonate of soda. Baking soda makes the dioxide gas bubbles that make Hokey Pokey bubble up.

Baste: Spoon or brush the juices and marinade over meat or poultry during roasting to keep it moist.

Batch: A quantity of food made at one time, such as a batch of biscuits or cookies.

Batter: An uncooked mixture that is thin enough to pour, usually has egg, flour and a liquid, like pancake batter.

Beat: Mix ingredients together by stirring vigorously, usually with a wire whisk or electric mixer.

Blanch: Briefly put food into boiling water without cooking it – used to remove skins from tomatoes.

Blend: Mix ingredients thoroughly, or mix ingredients in an electric blender.

Boil: Heat a liquid until bubbles keep rising and breaking on the surface.

Chill: Put in the refrigerator until cold.

Chop: Cut food into small, uneven pieces. Coarsely chopped is big pieces, finely chopped is small pieces.

Combine: Mix ingredients together.

Cream: Beat together butter and sugar until the mixture is pale and fluffy and looks a bit like whipped cream.

Dice: Cut into small cubes.

Dough: An uncooked mixture soft enough to be worked with the hands but too stiff to pour, like bread dough.

Drain: Pour off liquid, generally by putting it through a strainer or colander.

Dust: To cover very lightly with a flour or icing sugar. Icing sugar is often sprinkled or dusted over cakes or muffins before serving.

Fry: Cook food in hot fat or oil.

Garnish: Decoration, not necessarily edible, added to the finished dish to make it look nice. Parsley is the most common garnish.

Grate: Rub against a grater to shred into small pieces.

Grease: Rub the surface of a tray or cake tin with butter or oil to stop the mixture from sticking during cooking.

Knead: Work dough with the heel of your hand.

Marinate: Soak meat or poultry in a mixture of oil, vinegar, citrus juice or wine and flavourings to make it tender and add flavour.

Melt: Heat a solid, such as butter, until it becomes liquid.

Pinch: The amount of dry ingredient that you can pick up between your thumb and forefinger.

Poach: Cook food gently in liquid at the simmer point, so that the surface of the liquid is just below boiling point.

Preheat: Heat the oven up before putting the food in. It usually takes about 15 minutes for an oven to come up to baking temperature.

Sift: Shake dry ingredients through a sieve to get a soft, airy texture and remove any lumps or impurities.

Stir-fry: Quick method of frying in a little fat. The food must be cut into small pieces and moved around until cooked. Usually done in a wok over a high heat.

Zest: The brightly coloured outer layer of peel of a citrus fruit such as an orange or lemon.

Recipe Index

Happy cooking!

A RANDOM HOUSE BOOK
published by
Random House New Zealand
18 Poland Road, Glenfield, Auckland, New Zealand
www.randomhouse.co.nz

First published 2001
© 2001 EZPZ Corporation Ltd, Jo Seagar & John Stringer
The moral rights of the authors have been asserted
ISBN 1 86941 491 8

Cover and text design: Sharon Grace, Grace Design
Project management: Barbara Nielsen, Stylus Publishing Services
Front cover photograph: Jae Frew
Printed by Wyatt & Wilson